NAMIBIA
A VISUAL CELEBRATION

CONTENTS

Page 1 The quiver tree, indigenous to Namibia, belongs to the aloe family. Its hollow trunk and branches were used by the San to fashion quivers (hence the name). Here in the Quiver Tree Forest just outside Keetmanshoop, the late afternoon light turns the bark orange and velvety, its ridges forming a patchwork.

Previous spread On Kanaän, a farm between the Namib-Naukluft Park and the Tiras Mountains, we beat the sunrise. The reward is this surreal light – saturated reds and blues and blacks.

Left One of the best-known plants in the Kalahari, the camelthorn tree is protected by law. This gnarled and sprawling specimen in the Namib-Naukluft Park seems ancient and otherworldly, reaching out to clutch the sky with branches as fine as filigree.

INTRODUCTION

Namibia will haunt you. It will take a piece of you and change it. It is impossible to know beforehand how or where it will happen, but whether in the chilly, mysterious desert mists of Swakopmund, in the lone tracks of a brown hyena in the dunes or in the ghostly silence of Sossusvlei's ancient dunes, it will find a way into you. For good.

The tone of the Namibian geography can move even the most jaded traveller with its large, sighing sights. Times and places for introspection abound. Yes, this country is one massive vacation of the mind. Add the Namibian people to the equation and you begin to realise that this is a truly special place.

The Namibians inhabit just a handful of medium-sized towns – even the capital, Windhoek, has a business district reminiscent of a suburb in a big city – and a smattering of smaller towns, mostly in the interior. There is also a large rural population on commercial farms and those on tribal land in the north, like the pastoral Himba. The people who call this home have come from everywhere. Some may have been here since the dawn of time, others came from the north and from Africa's great lakes, some migrated from the south and still others arrived by sea from Europe.

The San (Bushmen) may be its most famous residents, but the Herero – the women often postcarded in their characteristic colourful Victorian-era dresses and headgear – are equally recognisable. The Khoi-speaking Nama and Damara are not far behind with these fashions, while the biggest population groups – the Owambo

Left On Kanaän, a farm between the Namib-Naukluft Park and the Tiras Mountains, an ostrich egg lies amidst the feathery, spreading seed stalks of the grass.

Right A quiver tree shows off its unique shape, outlined in black against the setting sun.

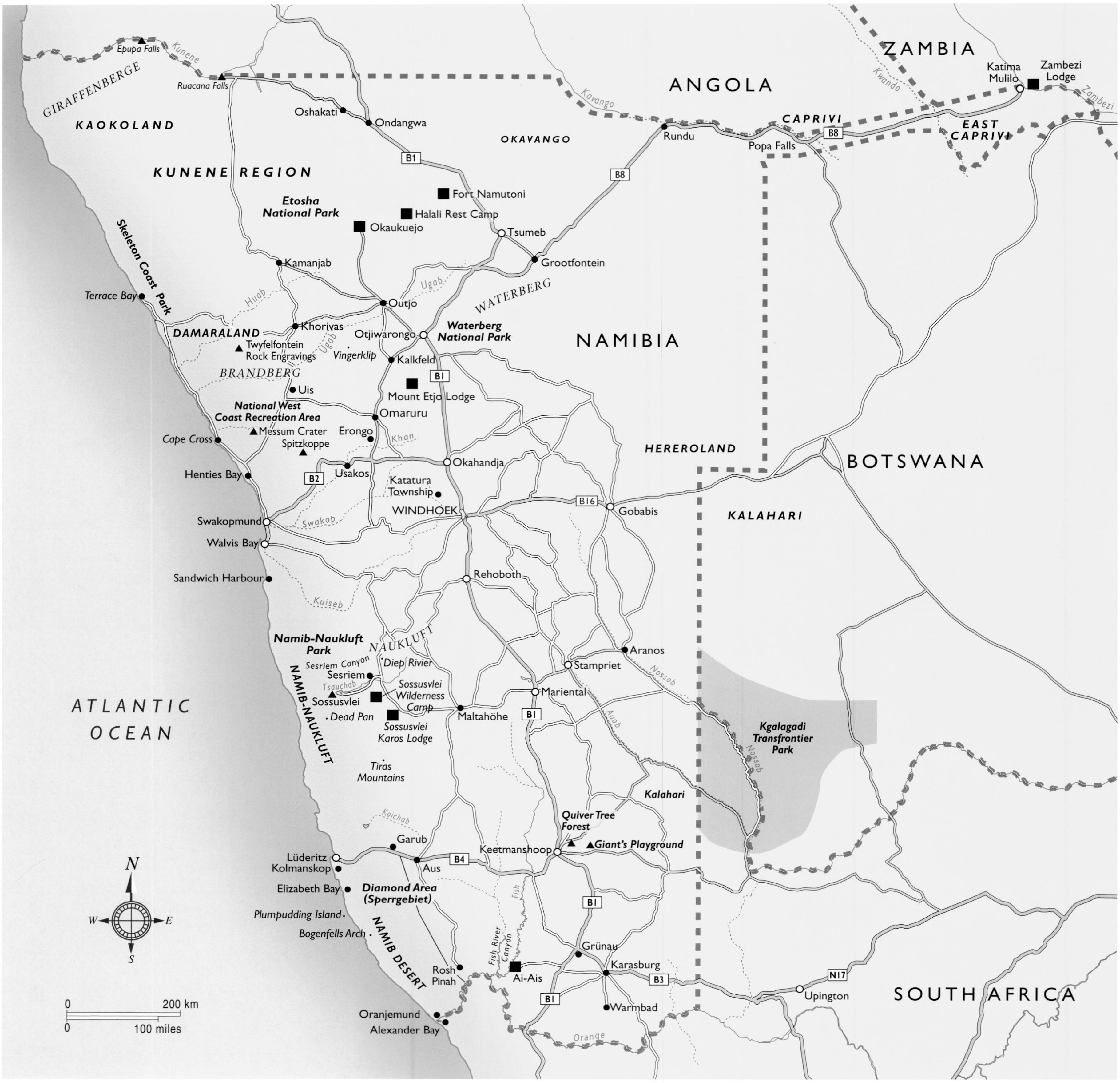
ZAMBIA
ANGOLA
NAMIBIA
BOTSWANA
SOUTH AFRICA
ATLANTIC OCEAN
Epupa Falls
Kunene
Ruacana Falls
GIRAFFENBERGE
KAOKOLAND
Oshakati
Ondangwa
OKAVANGO
Kavango
Rundu
CAPRIVI
Popa Falls
B8
Kwando
Katima Mulilo
Zambezi Lodge
Zambezi
EAST CAPRIVI
B1
KUNENE REGION
Fort Namutoni
Etosha National Park
Halali Rest Camp
Okaukuejo
Tsumeb
Skeleton Coast Park
Kamanjab
Grootfontein
Terrace Bay
Huab
Ugab
Outjo
WATERBERG
DAMARALAND
Khorixas
Otjiwarongo
Waterberg National Park
Twyfelfontein Rock Engravings
Vingerklip
Kalkfeld
BRANDBERG
Uis
Mount Etjo Lodge
National West Coast Recreation Area
Omaruru
Messum Crater
Erongo
Cape Cross
Spitzkoppe
Khan
HEREROLAND
Okahandja
Henties Bay
B2
Usakos
Katatura Township
B16
Gobabis
Swakopmund
Swakop
WINDHOEK
KALAHARI
Walvis Bay
Rehoboth
Sandwich Harbour
Kuiseb
Namib-Naukluft Park
NAUKLUFT
Aranos
Sesriem Canyon
Diep Rivier
Stampriet
Sesriem
Nossob
Tsauchab
Sossusvlei Wilderness Camp
Mariental
Sossusvlei
Maltahöhe
Dead Pan
Sossusvlei Karos Lodge
Auob
Kgalagadi Transfrontier Park
NAMIB-NAUKLUFT
Tiras Mountains
Kalahari
Koichab
Quiver Tree Forest
Giant's Playground
Garub
Lüderitz
Keetmanshoop
Kolmanskop
Aus
B4
Elizabeth Bay
Diamond Area (Sperrgebiet)
Fish
Plumpudding Island
NAMIB DESERT
Bogenfells Arch
Fish River Canyon
Grünau
Rosh Pinah
Ai-Ais
Karasburg
B3
N17
Upington
Warmbad
Oranjemund
Alexander Bay
Orange
N
W
E
S
0
200 km
0
100 miles

(who constitute almost half the population), the Caprivians and the Kavango – speak Bantu languages. Afrikaans, English and German are commonly spoken, and not just by the white population, which is largely made up of German and South African expatriates. The Basters of Rehoboth speak Afrikaans, as do many of the coloured groups.

With all this racial diversity, Namibia sounds complicated and potentially volatile, but the opposite is true. Especially since gaining full independence in 1990, the country has been peaceful, its people intermingling (and marrying) freely, their hospitality extending to any visitors from both near and far.

Seldom can the term 'vastness' be more aptly used than to describe this Southern African country. With its hot, sandy western side up against the cold Atlantic, it slots in snugly atop South Africa, which is to the south, with Angola to the north and Botswana to the east. It looks like a solid, manageable block of land, except for that strange 'finger' sticking out towards Zambia. That is the Caprivi Strip, product of the last days of the 'scramble for Africa', when Britain chopped a piece off Bechuanaland (now Botswana) and gave it to Germany in exchange for Zanzibar.

Like so many modern African countries, Namibia's borders are a legacy of colonial times, but its history goes back so far that any period of dominance or imposed rule by a European country seems almost incidental, and fleeting at that.

Namibia's tourist brochures portray none of the more conventional holiday imagery, like honeymoon couples on white beaches with swaying palm trees above. A large part of Namibia's coast is known as the Skeleton Coast, and is littered with centuries of shipwrecks. Very few habitations line the shore and even the most charming of them, like Lüderitz, are more often than not wind-blown and desolate places.

Herein lies the allure of the country. It seems impenetrable and hostile, but once you start exploring, you realise it is the exact opposite. As the land lies stretched in every direction – sometimes jagged, barren outcrops, sometimes thorny savannah, sometimes blistering red desert sands – it promises nothing right to the horizon where, once reached, the same vista will endlessly repeat itself, maybe with slight variations.

But find a town, or just a habitation – maybe a farmer's homestead – and you will find people willing to share every aspect of their lives, people shaped by this severe land and its extreme weather. Just under two million people live here, but in an area of 824 292 km² (bigger than the United Kingdom and France put together), they disappear almost completely.

This luxury of space is Namibia's biggest drawcard. Yes, its star attraction is its absence of distractions. You could travel one of the major highways all day long and encounter only a handful of cars. As if revelling in the space available to them, the country's tourist attractions are equally enormous. From the wildly eroded Fish River Canyon in the south to the vast Etosha Pan in the north, the geographical features spill over the canvas in front of you as if competing to impress.

There are no half-measures when it comes to the weather either. While the temperatures are much more bearable during the winter months, Namibia has for

Page 10, top On the border of the Namib-Naukluft Park, a dead quiver tree seems to stand guard where two worlds meet, the above one cold and damp, while below the landscape is softened by the setting sun.

Page 10, bottom The desert reclaims everything, including this car, left over from diamond-rush days and abandoned between Lüderitz and Walvis Bay.

Page 11 In the diamond area near Lüderitz, it is possible to stand in the desert and look out towards the blue stillness of the sea. This picture was taken through Bogenfels Rock Arch.

the best part of the year, a hot, dry climate. The ocean is cold enough to relegate swimming to being a niche activity, while the wind in places like Walvis Bay lures windsurfers from across the world. It is the sun, however, that you will remember – a sun that will make you appreciate shade like never before. Summer thunderstorms occur and, when the fat, blue-and-white clouds release their bounty on the land, the effect is instantaneous: grass grows where previously there was only sand, trees push green from their slumbering branches and overnight the landscape turns into a short-lived land of plenty.

Namibia is a country of contrasts, where elephants survive in near-desert conditions, where enormous flocks of flamingos paint pink swathes in the most unlikely places and where people thrive against all odds. Its beauty is raw and unpolluted, its days brightly lit by a seldom-wavering sun, the nights frequently clear and ablaze with stars.

Convention calls lush green gardens beautiful. Namibia is a garden of rock and sand and bizarre plants, plentiful antelope and predators. A savage, raw, parched beauty, but beauty like nowhere else you have ever been before.

Above Dawn at Sesriem, and this great hot-air balloon carrying tourists rises into cotton-candy clouds to waft for a few hours above the desert. All around, the scene is brushed with the pink of a rising sun.

Opposite Sunset on Kanaän and a coming-together of cloud, fading light, tree and sky creates an almost surreal display.

Overleaf The Dead Pan in Sossusvlei is a white, dry, cracked lake, with strange and ancient camelthorns as black as if they had been burnt.

THE SOUTHERN REGION

The southern part of the country consists of the administrative regions of Hardap and Karas. Karasburg and Grünau are the first major towns en route from South Africa, then Keetmanshoop, Mariental and Rehoboth follow on the B1 highway northwards, which runs straight up over the high central plateau, crossing the Tropic of Capricorn neatly just south of Rehoboth.

From this plateau, where much of the country's premier commercial farmland lies, the landscape drops off sharply to the west towards the Namib Desert and tapers off eastwards, somewhat listlessly, towards the Kalahari Desert, Botswana and the Kgalagadi Transfrontier Park.

The southern border is formed by the slow, brown Orange River. This offers leisurely drives on its banks and canoeing all the way to the Sperrgebiet ('prohibited area'), which starts near the mining town of Rosh Pinah. There the iconic quiver trees can be seen as solitary silhouettes or small clusters, like families posing for a hasty photograph.

When approaching Lüderitz from the interior, the road drops down the Huib-Hoch Plateau, the realm of Namibia's famous wild desert horses. Nothing, however, can prepare you for the plunge into the innards of the earth that is the Fish River Canyon. This view point near Hobas is one of the country's many sacred places.

The Namib is one of the oldest, driest deserts in the world (average rainfall: 10 mm). A large part of it is protected by the Namib-Naukluft Park, where the dunes, pans and trees of the Sossusvlei area make up some of the Namib's most famous scenes.

Left Roads in this country run forever. On the way to Aus, clouds are gathering over the mountains and the unusually long grass beside the road looks white-gold and green.

Right Two ground squirrels look at the camera at the same time, a shot that took five hours in 40°C heat to capture.

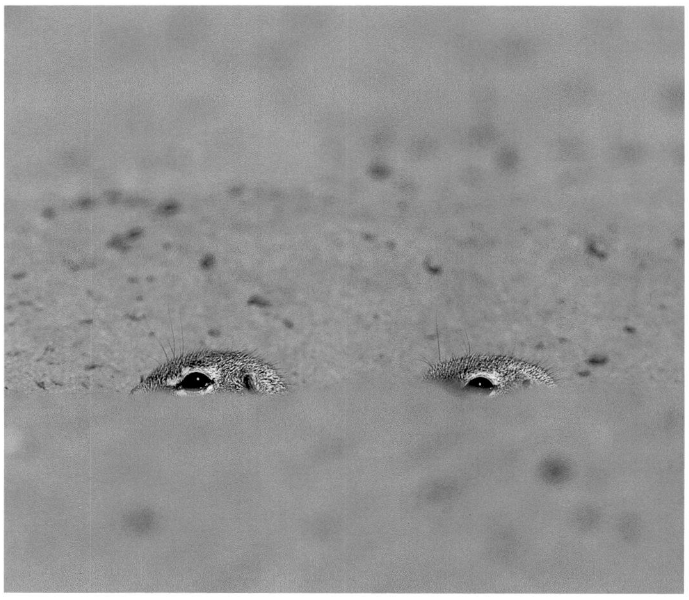

Above Established in the 1900s, Kolmanskop was once a prosperous and thriving town, with its own casino and playhouse, and a hospital with the first x-ray machine in the southern hemisphere. Fifty years later it was dead. The diamond rush moved south and the desert moved in, slipping through doors and windows to occupy the once-genteel rooms.

Left In the shabby, windswept grandeur of these great houses there is a haunting feeling of former occupation, of voices faintly heard in passageways, speaking of better days. The sun streams through paneless windows, warping the floors.

POMONA
0.8.191

Opposite top A ghost house in Pomona, south of Lüderitz. With the clouds gathering eerily above it and the empty house looming out of the sand, there is a sense of foreboding here.

Opposite bottom Shuttered and bolted, this house seems set to withstand the onslaught of the desert.

Above Built in 1911, the Lutheran Felsenkirche ('church on the rocks') towers above Lüderitz, its minister still actively serving some 20 000 people.

Above In Dead Pan after good rains, the scrubby grass makes a rare appearance. Although it is early in the day, the sun is already blazing, and the dead camelthorn tree outlined half against sky, half against dune, stands solitary under the unforgiving sun.

Left Before sunrise, the Dead Pan is a magical place. The dead trees are like dancers striking poses, and the cracked, dry lake floor looks almost like water, as it shimmers blue in the early morning light. Soft shadows retreat across the dunes, blurred against the light sky.

Above Sunset in the Quiver Tree Forest and the scene is calm, shot with purple, deepening to black. The trees seem like regal elders circling around, gathering in closer for the night, as the earth breathes out in the lingering tendrils of daylight.

Right As the rain clouds gather, the Quiver Tree Forest changes rapidly – a dark, desolate landscape where a sense of foreboding lurks, heralded by the heavy skies.

Opposite In the desert only the smartest and hardiest survive. This agama lizard seems precariously perched on flimsy branches, but it has been there for hours, happily unmoving, soaking up the sun.

Above A tortoise emerges from the cool of its shell to greet a fellow desert traveller.

Right An ant highway, a few centimetres wide, hard and slippery as soap, is etched into the desert floor. In the desert, survival for the largest and smallest depends on following the right roads – and the ants are no exception.

Overleaf Moving gracefully between bushes this cobra is reminiscent of DH Lawrence's majestic poem 'Snake'. It is unusually tolerant of the camera, which is about a metre away.

Above A 4x4 is a standard working vehicle in the Kalahari – how else to negotiate the dongas and dips, and the acres and acres of land on these massive farms?

Opposite A sand shower rains down on passengers as the wheels of the truck dig in unexpectedly on an incline.

TOYOTA

Above The horizon curves between two camelthorn trees, scrubby bushes echo scrubby clouds. Under the not-quite-blue sky, anchored in the red dust, one of the trees seems deformed by the huge weavers' nests built into its branches.

Right At the end of a stormy day, a rainbow, like a double promise, seems to imbue our deformed tree with strange and special properties, a magic tree on a magic plain.

Overleaf Like a Rorschach ink-blot, the massive nest throws up different images for different people. One sees a horse's head formed in the shadow, someone else sees a baboon.

Above Near Sesriem stands Elim Dune with its deep ochre sands and its prepossessing height. From the top the view goes on for miles, not only of the desert, but also across velvety grasslands, green and golden, to the suggestion of mountains on the far horizon.

Left At the edge of the Namib Desert, this petrified sand-dune looks out towards the far mountains. In between, the shadows and soft light turn the scrubby grass to a rich, golden pelt, and the sky whitens.

Above A most unusual Namibian landscape. Like a Pierneef painting, craggy purple mountains, which would be more at home in the Boland, rise in the distance – and, in the foreground, bountiful rains have led to green grass where there should be desert scrub.
Left Later in the year, the desert climate takes its toll. Grass dries out and the earth reasserts itself.
Overleaf Ironically, in Namibia, most roads seem to pass through Solitaire – and this one is no exception. All around, the vista is unseasonably green, the skies above heavy with cloud before the rain.

Above The view across to the Tiras Mountains, with rain falling heavily all around and the sun just breaking through clouds to cast a skein of light across the valley, makes this feel like a dreamscape. It is stormy and dramatic, but slightly unreal, and seems protected by the rainbow. In the centre the earth turns to gold.

Right The very next evening, the rain has cleared and the land is awash with colour as palettes run fluidly into one another. Looking towards the Tiras, this landscape is gentler, calmer, as rolling oranges fade to gold and green, and rose skies turn to lilac, touching the soft shadows of mountains.

Above The rain has brought miraculous changes. There are grasslands like wheatfields, green as the Overberg for as far as the eye can see, and a softer light. This is the gentle face of Namibia – and it is not the usual one.

Left Six months later and the green has turned to gold as the grass runs to seed and becomes patchy and dry. The light, too, is different as Namibia heads into the dry season – everything is harder and sharper as the land's true character reasserts itself.

Overleaf Some of the geological formations in Namibia date back more than 2 000 million years, and these fossils at Keetmanshoop fill one with a sense of awe. Some prehistoric, reptilian thing that crawled this planet long before man has left its mark in this rock, its claws reaching out like fingers from the past.

This spread From this hill near Keetmanshoop the world seems flat, but the changes in the sky can make all the difference between one shot and the next. These two landscapes, taken a few days apart from the same place, look vastly different. The first is touched with blue, and rich, the carpet of brush on the floor as thick as a sheep's pelt. The second, with its muted hues of rose and fuchsia fading to deeper purples, is ethereal, somehow less substantial.

Above These formations at Giant's Playground were caused by the erosion of sedimentary overlying rocks 170 million years ago – huge basalt blocks balanced haphazardly on top of each other, as if piled on by the hand of some enormous, invisible Goliath, toying with them for his own amusement. It is almost impossible to understand the scale of these rocks, the marvellous, dangerous balancing acts. Against the cerulean blue of the sky, they seem to teeter between the quiver trees. This strange area is vast and disconcerting.

Opposite There is no moon, so the shutter is left open for eight hours overnight. The camera captures the movement of stars as the earth turns: a whirlwind of light, with the camera at the centre.

Right A desert adder, fat and lethal, is camouflaged among the stones, just waiting to be stepped on.

Overleaf In Solitaire, the one-horse town through which the world passes, a rusted car becomes a feature, posed among the cacti near a defunct petrol pump. In the background is the only accommodation for miles around.

SOLITAIRE
COUNTRY LODGE

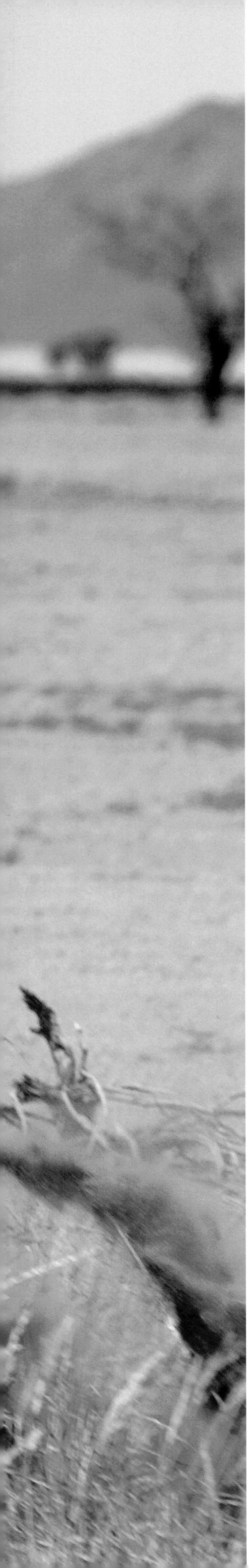

Left A gemsbox (oryx) on the run, its enormous hindquarters powering it onwards, muscles bunching and flexing, leaving swirling red dust in its wake.

Above Lynxes are beautiful but lethal, and can kill up to 200 sheep in a single night.

Overleaf A troop of ostriches moves in formation across the grassland. They progress with a strange, ungainly grace, loping rather than running, seemingly heading for nowhere in particular.

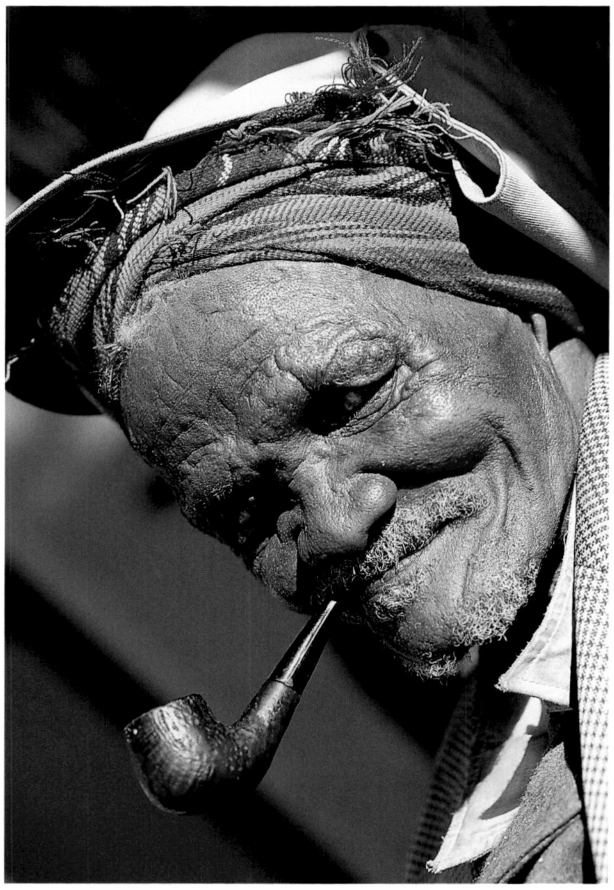

Above To live in this hard land, you need to become hard too. This *Skaapwachter* (shepherd), with his flock of pitch black karakuls and his roguish smile, survives out here in the middle of nowhere, travelling with his sheep, sleeping on the ground.

Left Ou Piet is a bit of an institution around Keetmanshoop – with his craggy face, the ubiquitous pipe clamped between his teeth, and a colourful headscarf. No one is quite sure just how old he is, and legends about him abound.

Opposite A mother and son wait at the side of the road between Keetmanshoop and the Quiver Tree Forest. All neatly turned out for some special occasion, they point to their home in the distance.

Opposite At Garub in the Namib-Naukluft Park, wild horses fight. They are famous – the only herd of wild horses in any desert in the world – and the government maintains the waterhole at Garub especially for them. There are constant scuffles for leadership between the males.

Above The wild horses seem unmmoved by the dramatic backdrop, where the koppies catch both sunlight and lightning as the sky grows heavier.

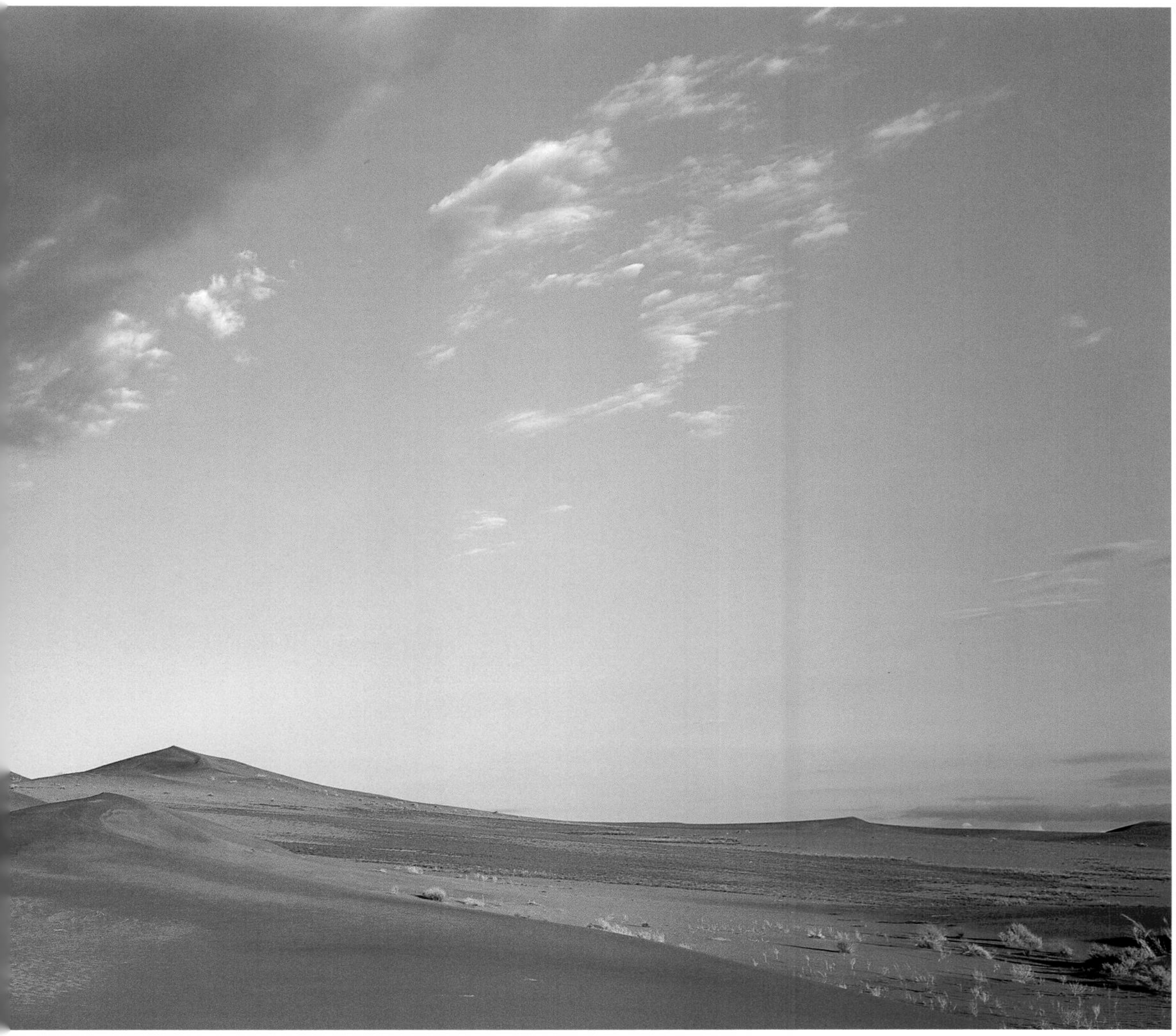

Above In Sossusvlei the setting sun casts the shadow of this camelthorn across the red face of a dune – the image is a strange distorted echo, like an old man's gnarled hand.

Left In the Namib-Naukluft Park, the clouds pull away towards the horizon, the earth curves, the desert stretches unending on either side.

Opposite top Rainfall in the desert brings colour where before there was only sand. These bright pink and purple flowers appear unexpectedly, strangely incongruous against the red earth.

Opposite bottom These succulents lie scattered across the desert floor, looking like small pebbles, until they pop open to reveal bright white flowers.

Above In the desert there is so little for plants to live on that they need to be able to take nourishment almost out of the air. This aloe stands tall and red in the fading light, and the clouds seem to flock to it, drawing the eye to its outline against the desert sky.

Above Cheetahs such as this one seen on a farm in Keetmanshoop are regarded as pests by farmers. They are now protected in national parks.

Left This cricket is as long as a man's hand and gives off a foul-smelling liquid when threatened.

Opposite A family of meerkats, voyeurs of the veld.

Overleaf Framed through the arms of a camelthorn tree on Kanaän, this scene shows the grass as it fades and runs to seed at the approach of the dry season. The air is still moist after rain, the sky is painted with a miracle of colours from pearl grey to pink, and the earth spreads out like a rich carpet of pale green and gold.

THE CENTRAL REGION

The northern central part of Namibia is its most populous and is centred around the capital, Windhoek. This region was known to the Khoisan, Nama and Herero for its hot springs (today in the suburb of Klein Windhoek), but the first permanent settlers here were the Oorlam under their leader Jonker Afrikaner in about 1840. By 1842, Rhenish missionaries had arrived and in 1890 the German military started paving the way for the first wave of German colonists. It was only in 1909, however, that Windhoek became a proper municipality.

From the air Windhoek resembles jagged roof tiles squeezed in between impressive mountains – some of the highest peaks in Namibia. It is the ideal starting point for your exploration – from here, you can gradually venture further and further into the disparate corners of the country.

The small Daan Viljoen Game Park just outside the city is the perfect place for a leisurely game drive, and some of the region's endemic birds, such as the Damara rock-jumper, Montiero's hornbill and Rüppel's parrot, can be seen here.

The B6 highway heads out of Windhoek due east via Gobabis towards Botswana. The going is slower west of the city, with roads winding through the Khomas Hochland Mountains. The Us, Bosua, Kupferberg, Gamsberg and Kuiseb passes are some of the most scenic along the route.

North and north-east of the capital the towns of Usakos, Karibib and Okahandja all lie on the main B2 route towards Swakopmund. If you head straight north through the savannah vegetation characteristic of the Namibian interior, you will reach Otjiwarongo, where the central plateau starts flattening out.

Left These painstakingly crafted and hand-painted wares, the primary source of income for hundreds of citizens, are displayed on cloths spread on the ground in Windhoek.

Right Sometimes the simplest things give the greatest pleasure. At the side of the road, this small girl devours a mealie.

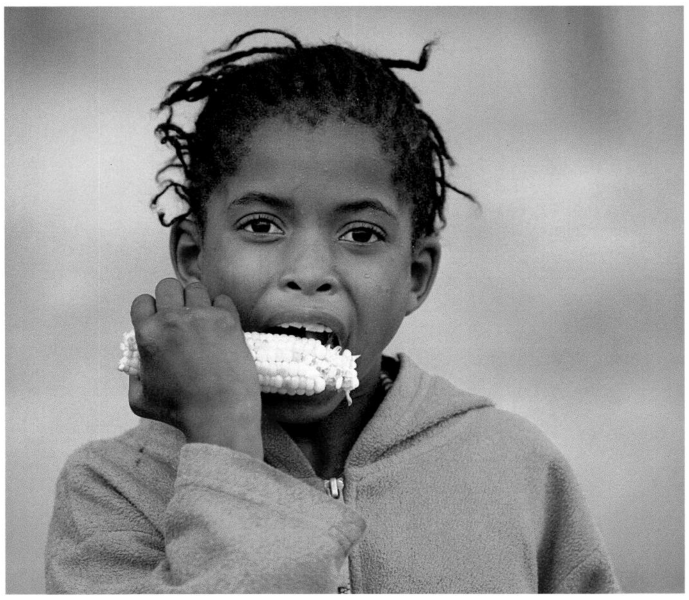

Previous spread Late at night, the 'Ruiter van Suidwes' ('Rider of Southwest' or 'Reiter Denkmal'), an equestrian memorial, stands guard over the centre of Windhoek. The Christuskirche, consecrated in 1910 and a mixture of neo-Romanesque and Gothic architecture, is lit with an ethereal light, its 42-metre steeple towering above the streetlamps.

Above From the Supreme Court, built in 1997, justice is dispensed to Windhoek's 20 000 inhabitants.

Left In Windhoek, old German architecture and modern skyscrapers are juxtaposed.

Opposite The entrance to the Christuskirche, which was constructed at a cost of DM 360 000 (double the original budget). Most of the material used for the church, including the marble in the elegant portico, was shipped from Italy or Germany – the only local contribution being sandstone.

Glory To The Fallen
Heroes And Heroines
of The Motherland
Namibia!
Sam Nujoma
26th August 2002

Opposite Sam Nujoma, Namibia's first democratically elected president and leader of SWAPO, the ruling party, erected this tribute to fallen comrades and the motherland: a statue of himself, armed and ready in full battle dress.

Above Old and new together – side by side, if not completely harmonious. One could be forgiven for thinking oneself in some small German town – if it weren't for the heat, of course.

Right An interesting angle on big-city buildings turns downtown Windhoek into a Miami street scene – with the skycrapers and the palm trees.

Above Taxidermy is big business in Namibia. Hunters want to take their trophies home, so a trade that is dying elsewhere attracts apprentices in Namibia. This dedicated pupil is practising on the head of a wildebeest.

Opposite One of Windhoek's colourful characters, Aaron Gotteillib, unofficial concierge at the Kalahari Sands. Ten years ago Aaron had only a few badges. Today, he is covered with them – and guests are always giving him more.

HANNOVER
Himmlischi Gschtaute
Hard Rock
FREE KUWAIT
21st March 1990
NAMIBIA
Independence Day
SUPER SAVINGS
SENTRA
SUPER SERVICE
UNTAG
YOUR VOTE IS SECRET
Arts Festival
rainbow
ARGENTINA 2006
Chirac
Stop it!
UNION YES
MOM
JESSE
JACKSON, JR.
For CONGRESS
Nov. 28
COFFEE
NO WORKEE
Try a Virgin Island
YOU TOO CAN EARN R1500 PER WEEK!
DON'T PANIC

Previous spread It is chilly in the early mornings, and these three children wrapped in their blankets at the side of the road were irresistible – giggly and squirmy and delighted to have their photo taken.

Opposite This child looks wise for her years, posing with her bottled water and windswept mop of hair outside the entrance gate to the Spitzkoppe.

Above These realistic and painstakingly carved vehicles are sold by woodcarvers along the roadside.

Opposite At Okahandja, north of Windhoek, this carver specialises in large sculptures. All his tools – a variety of picks and knives – are fashioned by hand. He lives and works at the side of the road, his wares too large to carry home.

Above A Himba man and woman, over 2.5 metres tall, every detail intricately carved, sanded to smoothness.

Overleaf Every carver has a different speciality – a trademark. This man carves faces into enormous hunks of wood.

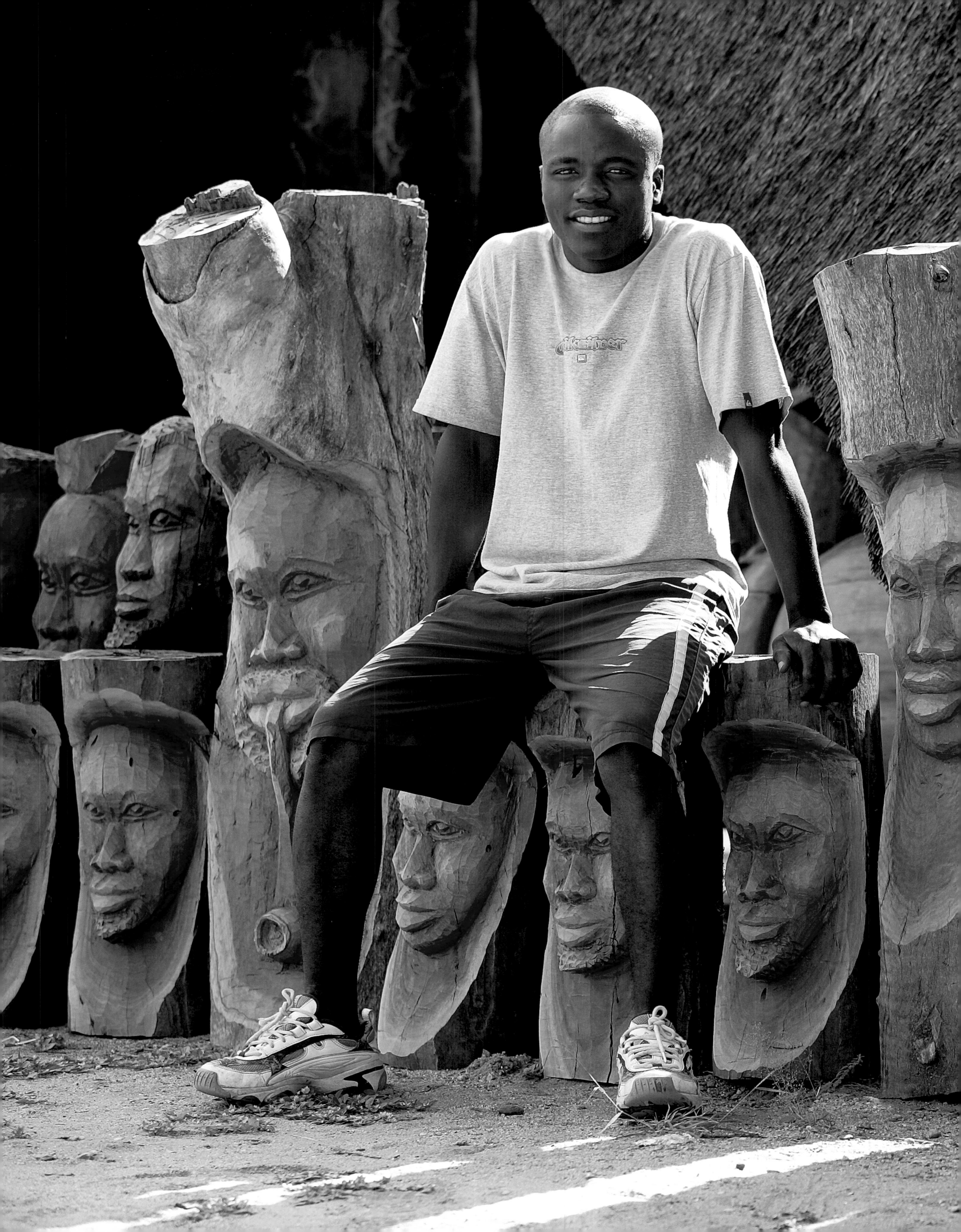

THE COASTAL REGION

From Foz do Cunene in the north to Oranjemund in the south, the Namibian coastline stretches almost uninterrupted for 1 400 kilometres. The only towns of any note are Henties Bay, Swakopmund, Walvis Bay and Lüderitz.

Future development will also be limited, not just by the extreme geography and climate, but also because the Sperrgebiet restricted diamond area, Namib-Naukluft Park and the Skeleton Coast Park in the north cover virtually the whole of the coastline.

Though this region has a low rainfall, the presence of the cold Benguela sea current causes a peculiar bank of thick fog, which can cover parts of the coast for up to 120 days of the year. This moisture is sufficient to support a remarkable diversity of life forms that call this desert coastline home. Some of these communities, like the lichen forests, are so minuscule that, to the untrained eye, they seem like nothing but windblown debris.

There are several colonies of Cape fur seals on the coastline, the most accessible being the Cape Cross colony and the one at Diaz Point near Lüderitz, where the remnants of a whaling station on Halifax Island are also visible.

The lagoons at Sandwich Harbour and Walvis Bay are the best places to see large flocks of flamingo, and massive, unwieldy pelicans jostling for space with hundreds of smaller waders.

The thin and fragile Namibian coastline is the delicate, cold counterpoint to a hot and dusty country. It is a buffer between the ocean behind you, and the vast unknown limits of this haunting and mysterious land.

Left A sea of seals at Walvis Bay. The scrabbling, scrapping, mewling mass of them is unbelievable as they huddle close to each other, knowing there is safety in numbers.

Right This young seal sleeps with the abandon of a child, sprawled and oblivious on his rock, certain that the grown-ups will be looking out for him.

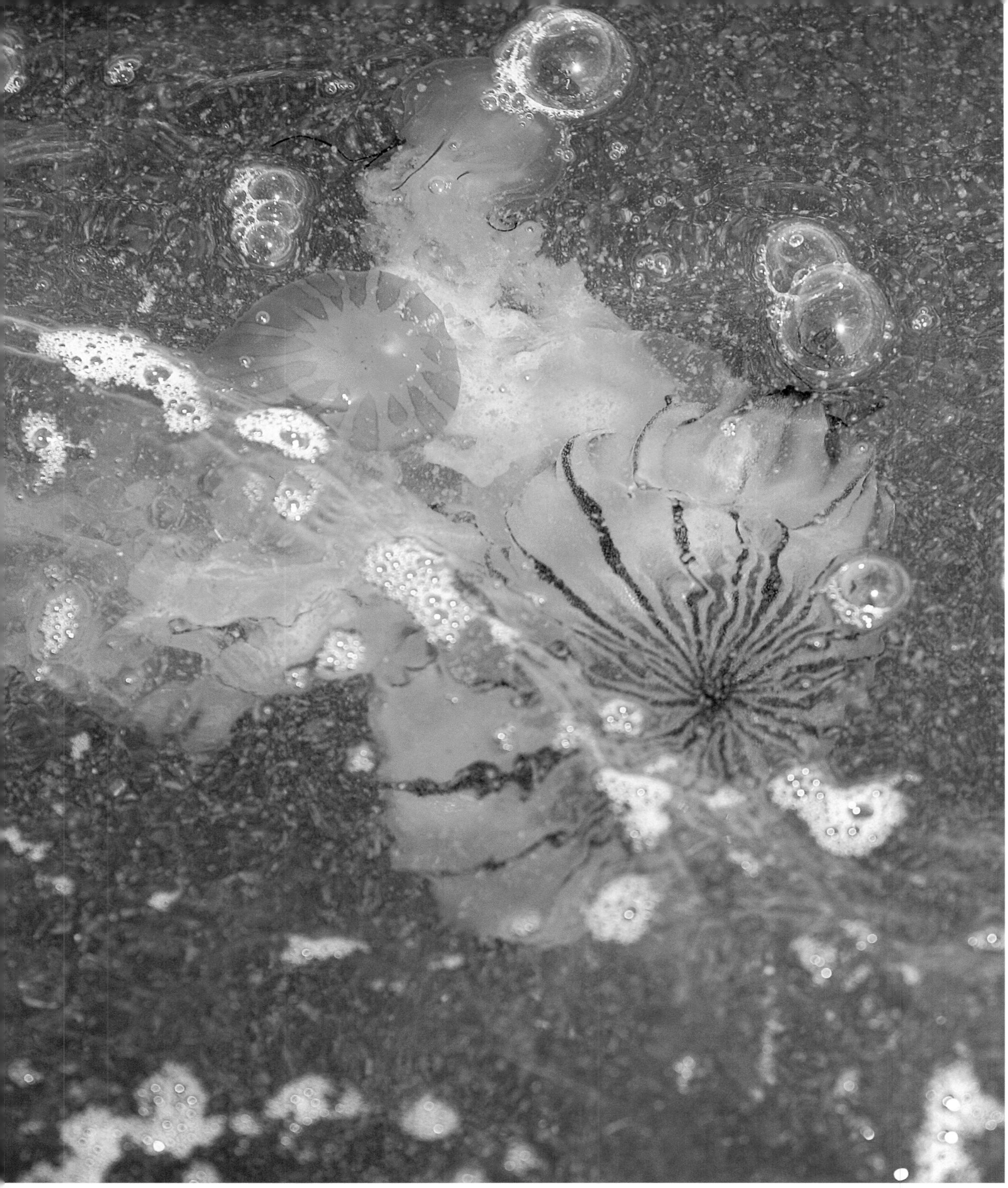

Above Over half a metre in diameter, this jellyfish is a semi-translucent mass of pink tentacles in the shallows.

Left A seal begs for fish from a boat.

Right At Cape Cross, Namibia's largest colony, this seal poses for the camera.

Overleaf, left An unfinished jetty provides perfect perches for the cormorants in Walvis Bay.

Overleaf, right (sequence) A leatherback turtle breaks the surface beside a boat after swimming alongside it beneath the surface for a while.

88
86
84
82
80
78
76
74
72
70
68
66
64
62
60
58
56
54
52
50

Page 94, top and bottom Pelicans are larger than they look, and even in the air they seem awkward and inelegant, the ugly ducklings of the sky.

Page 95 Seals take advantage of a new kind of island, colonising the bow of this ship as it stands in dock.

Left These painted benches in Swakopmund attract tourists with their carnival-like allure. Looking out onto the lighthouse, shaded by palms, this feels a bit like café society *à la* Med.

Above Fishing is not just for sport. This local resident cycles to the beach with his rods every day to catch supper for his family.

Opposite South of Walvis Bay, in the middle of the desert, is an unexpected Topnaar settlement. Diminutive descendents of the Khoikhoi, these desert people have eked out a life among the sands for over 3 000 years. Their history and their hardships line their faces, worn to leather by the Namib sun.

Above There are some 100 000 Herero people living in Namibia today. Unlike most African people, they favour a matriarchal society, with wealth passed down through the mother's line. With their distinctive headdresses and formal clothing, Herero women pride themselves on their appearance.

Right These budding entrepreneurs at the Spitzkoppe try to peddle rocks. Cash for their photo seemed like a fair exchange.

Above At Swakopmund airport, tourists queue for tandem jumps, accompanied by an experienced parachutist. Bright against the sky, the chutes circle above – and the landing is always accurate, strangely anti-climactic.

Right It is a bit like Independence Day out here in the desert. After the jump, the sense of exhilaration is almost tangible, making returning heroes of ordinary men.

Left In Swakopmund with its German heritage, beer is big. In this pub, youngsters take on a traditional five-litre flagon.

Above Camping out for the night, on top of the Rossingberg.

Previous spread The desert attracts all kinds of loners – nomads, explorers and, between Walvis Bay and Swakopmund, this daredevil on a quad bike creates his own sandstorm.

Above This palmato gecko survives in the desert by living just under the top layer of sand, which normalises its body temperature.

Right A lone motorcyclist on the road between Uis and Henties Bay has ridden up from Cape Town.

SHOEI
Z A

Above A moonscape of great granite inselbergs (island mountains). The Spitzkoppe are sculpted, softened and worn by the years, the weather and the sand.

Left It is hard to judge the scale of these hulking granite formations – but the seemingly tiny roads criss-crossing each other in the foreground give some idea.

Opposite Clouds scud by overhead and a sharp wind rustles through the golden grass. The light makes the Spitzkoppe seem softer, less imposing.

Above The rain moves in fast. It is still a few kilometres off, but the air is heavy, laden with water.

Right Etched against the blue sky, stark against the granite, this small tree somehow manages to survive, growing miraculously out of rock.

Above Dawn over the Spitzkoppe, and the scene is dreamlike. On the edges, remnants of darkness are still receding, and clouds from the night before still hover above. But the rising sun has already dusted the grass with gold, and the rock is softened by shadow as the world refreshes itself.

Left Only at first light are the granite hulks this colour, stained warm orange by the morning sun.

Overleaf A view out over the Spitzkoppe through 'The Window', as the rain clouds gather.

Right The 'Staatshuis' (Statehouse) in the middle of Swakopmund is flanked by palm trees, with the lighthouse illuminated as a backdrop. This scene seems slightly mystical and Arabic: a Moroccan fort guarding the port against pirates.

Overleaf In the early morning in Swakopmund, this reflection catches the classic dichotomy of old and new: the old municipal buildings caught in the vast, mirrored windows of the Crystal Palace.

1901
BEZIRKS GERICHT

1906
Altes Amtsgericht

THE NORTHERN REGION

The northern parts of Namibia are its wildest and most desolate, but also its most attractive, because of the allure of Etosha's wildlife and the scenic Damaraland, where the ancient rock engravings at Twyfelfontein bear testimony to times when this land was wetter and more fertile.

The northern border with Angola is formed by the Kunene River towards the Atlantic Ocean (only briefly interrupted by the Ruacana and Epupa falls) and by the Kavango River towards the east. At Divundu, the Kavango slices through the Caprivi Strip via the slight flutter of the Popa Falls towards Botswana in the south. The further east you drive along the Caprivi Strip, the more distant Windhoek becomes, so much so that, by the time you reach Katima Mulilo, you are closer to the capitals of Zambia and Botswana than you are to Windhoek.

The administrative region of Kunene covers the Kaokoland, where the famous desert elephants survive against all odds. The Kaokoland is the most sparsely populated part of the country and home of the Himba, a group related to the Herero.

The distribution area of the *Welwitschia mirabilis*, a desert plant that can lives for 1 000 years, starts in Damaraland around the Doros and Messum craters, then stretches down towards the arid gravel plains inland from Swakopmund.

Damaraland's geographical features belong in fantasy films. A rock formation called the Organ Pipes lie near Burnt Mountain, while a fossilised forest is scattered across a hillside some kilometres further on. The Finger Rock tickles the sky somewhere between Khorixas and Outjo and Brandberg and the Spitzkoppe shoot skywards from the arid landscape, static red rock billowing in the heat haze.

Left Etosha, late in the afternoon, and zebras drink as the setting sun reflects in the water.
Right A spike-heeled lark takes a break in its busy day.

Above The rib cage of a ship on the Skeleton Coast. The early Portuguese sailors called this wilderness of white sand – with its impenetrable fogs, violent storms and treacherous rocks – 'the coast of hell'. Later, faced with a coastline littered with skeletons just like this, the locals re-christened it.

Right Kaokoland, one of the last great wildernesses, where the desert meets the ocean. Those who survived shipwrecks and the torturous swim to shore faced an even greater threat: 300 kilometres of wild, coastal desert.

Opposite Softened and sandblasted as time wears on, bits and pieces of once-grand ships become abstract artefacts half-buried in the sand as the land slowly reclaims them.

Previous spread and opposite The Himba are a nomadic people who live for the most part in the north of Kaokoland. For more than 3 000 years, they have retained their culture and resisted any attempts to assimilate them into the rest of Namibian society.
Above From adolescence a Himba woman's hair is worn in elaborate dreadlocks. It is considered most beautiful once it reaches her shoulders. The women, their bodies smeared with butterfat, red ochre paste and herbs, seem to glow in the desert light.
Right The white conch shell is a sign that a Himba woman is married. The shells, called *ohumba*, are found only on the East Coast of Africa and are prized by the Himba, who will trade many goats for a specimen.

Previous spread This 20-centimetre chameleon is changing from yellow to green, either in response to stress or to regulate its temperature.

Above The San call Namibia 'the land God made in anger', and the Damaraland landscape lends credence to this belief, with its burnt-red earth and stark rock formations. Along the wall of what was once the Messum River, these strange outcrops resemble horses' heads.

Opposite Close to Twyfelfontein is the dolerite formation called the Organ Pipes. The site is thought to have been formed over a hundred million years ago by volcanic activity. The fast-cooling dolerite shrank into these strangely graceful and symmetrical columns.

Right The ground is unforgiving out here, but this small tree, twisted and insignificant as it looks, clings onto the rocks under a blazing sky. It is a sign that life triumphs, even in these harshest of conditions.

Opposite and above The Namib is the only place in the world where the *Welwitschia mirabilis* grows. With only two evergreen leaves, which sprout directly from the ground, the welwitschia lives on as little as 25 mm of rainfall a year, and yet it can grow between 10 and 20 cm every month. The oldest specimen is estimated to be around 2 000 years old.

Right A typical desert plant, this cactus sprouts flowers between its thorns.

Previous spread These newly hatched ostrich chicks look like punctuation marks wandering behind their father, almost lost in his shadow.

Opposite This northern black korhaan picks his way in stately fashion across the desert floor.

Above A flock of finches at Goas Waterhole in Etosha. They buzz in and out of the water, flapping in the shallows, calling to each other in a many-winged hustle and bustle.

Right This yellow-billed kite at Nebrowni ignores the skinny springbok that passes on its way to a waterhole.

Left This hare was well camouflaged. It seemed to have great confidence in its invisibility and waited, frozen, for the perceived danger to pass.

Above and top A juvenile pale chanting goshawk swallows a lizard head-first.

Previous spread Elephants seem almost human. These two, still caked in dirt from their mud bath, share an intimate moment. Travelling together across the heat of Etosha's pan, they seem a lonely pair, outcasts separated from their herd.
Opposite At the end of another day in the desert, the elephants stop to drink. This youngster sticks close to his elders, and they, in turn, flank him protectively.
Above Something may have spooked this herd, or they had been travelling a while and the scent of water was calling strongly: whatever the reason, they stormed their way towards the Okaukuejo waterhole.
Right Incongruously coy and dainty, this enormous, mud-caked elephant posed for a while with his legs crossed – first one, and then the other.

Previous spread A zebra mare and her colt exchange signs of affection, relaxed and content as the sun begins to set and the day cools around them.
Above This springbok drinks so daintily it hardly disturbs its own reflection.
Opposite top A gemsbok (oryx) wades in, slurping water with abandon.
Opposite bottom If they could speak, the hornbills would surely be the comedians of the veld. They are bright and spry and always watching, seeming to call out remarks, and chuckling to themselves in their own private language.

Previous spread These lion cubs are practising lying in wait for their prey – and with the confidence of the uninitiated they are pretty sure they are invisible.

Opposite This young lion is wooing his lady. She, unfortunately, does not seem interested.

Above Fresh from the waterhole, these wet cubs are play-fighting, jumping and tackling each other with such force that the droplets fly.

Overleaf Strangely gentle, these giraffes move elegantly towards the waterhole at Goas, shielding a baby in their midst.

Previous spread At Halali, this young jackal, fluffy at the edges, emerges at the end of the day after a few hours' sleep in a dark burrow. His small, sharp snout twitches in search of scents on the air.

Opposite top At Vingerklip (Finger Rock), looking out towards a great flat-topped rock island in the middle of nowhere, grey clouds gather and the sun slips away.

Opposite bottom On the edge of Etosha, this lone tree balances precariously. Beneath it, spread out like a still, white sea, the vast pan begins.

Above Sunrise in Etosha and the sun is caught between the black trunks of two camelthorn trees.

Overleaf Up close at Vingerklip lies a man-made pool under the ancient rock formation and the thunderous sky, with the desert scrub encroaching.

First edition published in 2007 by Struik Publishers
(a division of New Holland Publishing (South Africa) (Pty) Ltd)
New Holland Publishing is a member of Johnnic Communications Ltd

Garfield House
86–88 Edgware Road
W2 2EA London
United Kingdom
www.newhollandpublishers.com

Cornelis Struik House
80 McKenzie Street
Cape Town , 8001
South Africa
www.struik.co.za

14 Aquatic Drive
Frenchs Forest
NSW 2086
Australia

218 Lake Road
Northcote, Auckland
New Zealand

ISBN 9 781770 073623

Publishing Managers: Dominique le Roux and Felicity Nyikadzino Berold
Managing Editor: Lesley Hay-Whitton
Project Co-ordinator: Samantha Menezes-Fick
Designer: Martin Jones – Hirt & Carter Cape
Editor: Wendy Priilaid
Proofreader: Helen de Villiers

Reproduction by Hirt & Carter Cape (Pty) Ltd
Printed and bound by Tien Wah Press (Pte) Ltd

PHOTOGRAPHER'S ACKNOWLEDGEMENTS

Annatjie, my wife
Anja, my daughter
Donovan Cassisa
Helion von der Fecht – Walvis Bay
Johan (Rooies) and Eloma Cilliers – Keetmanshoop
Esterhuizen family: Andre, Simoné, Duan, Ampie and Charné – Namib Kalahari
Basie and Karin Oosthuizen – Swakopmund
Mike and Deon – Daredevil Adventures, Swakopmund
Hermie and Marlene Strauss – Kanaän
Coenie and Ingrid Nolte – Quiver Tree Forest and Giant's Playground, Keetmanshoop
Gino and Cathy Noli – Lüderitz
Fred and Astrid Deetlefs, Marco and Daniela Janse van Vuuren – Catamaran Charters, Walvis Bay
Petrus de Wet
Georgina Farrell
Pierre du Toit (very special friend and sherpa)

Left The Dead Pan in Sossusvlei.